Contents

Your admission

Support organisations

Introduction

Introduction

The Mental Health Act 2001 is the law that must be followed when giving care and treatment to people with mental illness. The Mental Health Commission wrote this booklet to tell you about your rights under that law.

Knowing the law will help you to know your rights.

The Act set up the Mental Health Commission. The job of the Mental Health Commission is to make sure that the law works properly to protect your rights and that services providing mental health care operate to the highest standards.

This booklet may answer the questions you have about mental health services and how you may receive treatment. This is general information only. You can discuss any questions you may have with any member of your care team.

Your friends, family members, carers and other people involved in your care may also find this booklet helpful. This information is also available in other languages on our website and in sign language.

Words we use in this booklet

Act
the Mental Health Act 2001

admission order
a form signed by a consultant psychiatrist to say that you must stay in hospital for care and treatment for 21 days

another consultant psychiatrist
a consultant psychiatrist (other than your own consultant psychiatrist) whom the Mental Health Commission appoints to independently examine you if you are involuntarily admitted to hospital

approved centre
a hospital or inpatient service that is registered by the Mental Health Commission

authorised officer
a member of staff of the Health Service Executive (HSE) authorised by the Chief Executive Officer of the HSE

care team
the doctors, nurses, consultant psychiatrists, clinical psychologists, social workers, occupational therapists, speech and language therapists and other mental health professionals who are involved in looking after you

general hospital
any hospital for general medical treatment that is not a mental health hospital, psychiatric hospital or psychiatric unit

hospital
in this booklet, the word 'hospital' means a mental health hospital (psychiatric hospital or unit) that you may stay in

law
in this booklet, the word 'law' always refers to the Mental Health Act 2001, which is the main law relating to mental health in Ireland

lawyer
a legal representative (solicitor or barrister) who will help you prepare for and will be at your mental health tribunal hearing

mental health services
includes home care, day hospitals, day centres, out-patient departments, in-patient departments, approved centres, community facilities and hostels or community residences

renewal order
a form signed by your consultant psychiatrist before your admission order ends to say that you must stay in hospital for another period of time

spouse
usually a husband or wife, but under the Act, also a man or woman living with a partner of the opposite sex continuously for three years or more

Mental health services and the law

Most people who have mental health problems are treated without going into hospital. Many people are treated by their GP or family doctor, who may refer them to specialist mental health services. Mental health care may be provided through home care, or at day hospitals, day centres or out-patient departments. Sometimes, you may need to go into hospital.

Most people who go into hospital for treatment do so by choice. This is called **voluntary admission**. However, people with mental disorders (see page 22 for the definition of a mental disorder) are sometimes admitted and treated against their will. This is called **involuntary admission**.

The law allows involuntary admission to hospital, but strict procedures must be followed for this to happen.

This booklet will explain:

- the procedures that must be followed if you are admitted to hospital against your will;

- the limited circumstances in which someone else can apply to have you admitted to hospital against your will;

- the steps that must be taken by everyone involved in the process for involuntary admission;

- what will happen once you are admitted to hospital; and

- **your rights** whether you are admitted as a voluntary patient or an involuntary patient.

Your rights

Your rights

The Mental Health Act 2001 makes sure your best interests are the most important aspect of mental health law. The Mental Health Act 2001 brings Irish law into line with international human rights standards.

The Act says that you have the right to receive good quality mental health care. Mental health services must be properly run and properly regulated. People working in the mental health services have to make sure that you are treated in a way that respects your rights as an individual. You should be treated with respect and dignity.

Your best interests

While you are using mental health services, your best interests should be considered before any decision about your care and treatment is made. You should be included in discussions with your care team about where your best interests lie to help you with your recovery.

Dignity and respect

According to the law, you have the right to be treated with dignity and respect. Your rights and best interests are central to any decision made about your care or treatment.

Your right to be fully informed

You have the right to be fully informed about your legal rights, your admission and treatment. You have a right to have everything explained to you. This information should be given in a way that you can understand. For example, if English is not your first language, the hospital may provide an interpreter if you need one. You should ask a member of your care team to explain any part of your care and treatment that you do not understand.

Your right to be listened to

You have the right to be listened to by all those working on your care team. You are entitled to take part in decisions that affect your health. Your care team should consider your views carefully.

Your right of review

If you are admitted involuntarily, a mental health tribunal will review your admission order or renewal order. The Mental Health Commission will make sure that you meet and are examined by another consultant psychiatrist who will prepare a report for the mental health tribunal. We will provide you with a lawyer, free of charge, to help you with the mental health tribunal. If you decide to appoint your own lawyer, you may have to pay their fees.

You must write to the Mental Health Commission if you are discharged before your mental health tribunal hearing but you would still like it to go ahead.

What does the Mental Health Act 2001 say?

The Act tells you:

O what a mental disorder is;

O why you may be admitted against your will to hospital;

O how you may be admitted against your will ('involuntary admission');

O where you may be admitted for psychiatric treatment or care;

O how you should be treated when you are admitted for psychiatric treatment or care; and

O what your rights are and what responsibilities your care team has towards you.

What does the Mental Health Act 2001 do?

- It gives you the right to automatically have your involuntary admission reviewed. This means that your case will be reviewed by an independent group of people called a mental health tribunal. For more information on mental health tribunals, please see page 59.

- It sets up the Mental Health Commission. For more information about us, please see page 71.

- It allows the Mental Health Commission to appoint the Inspector of Mental Health Services. For more information on the Inspector of Mental Health Services, see page 74.

What is a mental disorder?

You can only be admitted to hospital against your will if you have a mental disorder. For the first time in Ireland, the law defines mental disorder, as follows:

Disorder

- You have a mental illness, severe dementia or significant intellectual disability **and** there is a serious risk that you may cause immediate and serious harm to yourself or others.

or

- You have a mental illness, severe dementia or significant intellectual disability **and** your judgement is so impaired that your condition could get worse if you were not admitted to hospital for treatment that could only be given to you in hospital **and** going into hospital would be likely to improve your mental health significantly.

The following cannot be used as the only reason for stating that you have a mental disorder.

- You have a _personality disorder._ *?*

- You are socially deviant.

- You are addicted to drugs or toxic substances, for example alcohol.

what else would you need.

Your rights

Your admission

Your voluntary admission

Does the law affect me if I am a voluntary patient?

Most people who have mental health problems are treated without going into hospital. Most people who go to hospital for treatment do so by choice. If you are admitted, you will be known as a 'voluntary patient'.

As a user of the mental health services, your rights are protected under the law. Certain procedures must be followed when you are in hospital.

You may want to leave the hospital, but you should always discuss this with a member of your care team. If your doctor or nurse believes you are too ill to go home, they may decide it is in your best interest to stay.

If this happens, they can insist that you stay in hospital for up to 24 hours so that you can meet and be examined by your own consultant psychiatrist and a second consultant psychiatrist. You will only be admitted as an involuntary patient if both consultant psychiatrists decide that you have a mental disorder. See page 22 for the definition of a mental disorder.

If both consultant psychiatrists do not accept that you have a mental disorder, you may leave hospital or you may decide to stay as a voluntary patient.

Your involuntary admission

Questions and answers about involuntary admission

Can I be admitted to a hospital against my will?

Yes. Sometimes a person may have to be admitted for mental health treatment and care against their will. This is called 'involuntary admission'.

In what circumstances can I be admitted to hospital against my will?

You can only be admitted against your will if it is thought you meet the **conditions for involuntary admission**. These conditions are the rules set out in the law to make sure you are only admitted involuntarily if this is absolutely necessary. A mental health tribunal will review this decision.

What are the conditions for involuntary admission?

You can only be admitted involuntarily if you have a mental disorder. See page 22 for the definition of a mental disorder.

What are the procedures for involuntary admission?

The Act sets out the formal procedures that must be followed to admit you to hospital against your will as an involuntary patient. They are in three stages, as follows.

1. A person aged 18 or over can make an **application** to a doctor (in most cases this will be your GP) to have you admitted to hospital.

2. The doctor will examine you and if they think that you meet the conditions for involuntary admission, they will make a **recommendation** that you be admitted to hospital.

3. A consultant psychiatrist in the hospital will examine you. If they agree that you meet the conditions for involuntary admission, they will sign an **admission order**.

If you do not meet the conditions, the consultant psychiatrist will not sign the admission order. This means you will be free to leave the hospital. But it may be possible for you to stay in the hospital as a voluntary patient. You can discuss this option with a member of your care team.

How is an application made?

A person aged 18 or over can apply to have you admitted to hospital. This person is called the **applicant**.

The applicant fills in a form and gives it to a doctor. This doctor is usually your GP. This form asks the GP for a recommendation to admit you involuntarily. The applicant must have seen you during the 48 hours before making the application.

The applicant must tell the truth about their reasons for asking for you to be admitted to hospital. It is against the law for them to say anything about you that is not true.

The following people **can** make an application:

○ your spouse (see 'Words we use in this booklet', page 12);

○ an authorised officer (see 'Words we use in this booklet', page 10);

○ a member of the Gardaí; or

○ any other person aged 18 or over, **except** for those on the next list.

The following people **cannot** make an application to have you admitted involuntarily:

○ certain members of the Health Service Executive (formerly the Health Board) who are related to you or your spouse;

○ a member of the Gardaí who is related to you or your spouse;

○ any person who works at or for the hospital where you may be admitted;

○ a person who has a financial interest in the hospital where you may be admitted;

○ a spouse, parent, grandparent, brother, sister, uncle or aunt of any of the above people;

○ a person who is under 18 years of age;

○ your husband or wife who is living apart from you or who has had an application or 'barring' order made against them under the Domestic Violence Act, 1996.

Possible involvement of the Gardaí

There may be times when the Gardaí can make an application as part of their job.

The Gardaí have the power to take you into custody if they believe that you have a mental disorder and because of that mental disorder you may harm yourself or others.

If the Gardaí take you into custody, they must immediately arrange for you to be examined by a doctor. If the doctor thinks that you have a mental disorder, they will make a recommendation that you be admitted to hospital. The Gardaí will then bring you to the hospital that the doctor recommends.

If the doctor thinks that you do not have a mental disorder, you will be released immediately.

How is a recommendation made?

The doctor must meet and examine you within 24 hours of receiving the application form from the applicant. They may visit you at home or you can visit them in their surgery. They will explain why they are examining you unless they think it would not be good for your mental health.

In particular, the doctor will examine your behaviour, mood and thought processes.

If the doctor thinks that you meet the conditions for involuntary admission, they will make a recommendation to admit you to hospital for mental health care and treatment.

The doctor will fill out a **recommendation form**.

A copy of the recommendation form will be given to the applicant (the person who asked the doctor to examine you).

The doctor will tell you what hospital you might be admitted to.

If the doctor does not think you meet the conditions for involuntary admission, they will **not** fill in a recommendation form.

The applicant can go to another doctor and ask them for a recommendation. If the applicant goes to a new doctor, they **must** tell the new doctor that you were already examined by another doctor. They must tell the new doctor that the other doctor refused to fill in the recommendation form. It is against the law for the applicant not to say this to the new doctor.

What type of hospital will I be admitted to?

You will only stay in a hospital that is approved by the Mental Health Commission. These are known as **approved centres**. There are a number of approved centres around the country.

How will I be brought to the hospital?

The applicant should bring you. If this is not possible, your doctor will make arrangements with the clinical director of the hospital for hospital staff to collect you. The clinical director is the consultant psychiatrist in charge of the hospital.

If the clinical director and your doctor think that you may harm yourself or others, they may ask the Gardaí to help staff bring you to the hospital.

What happens when I arrive?

When you arrive at the hospital you will be under the care of a doctor or a nurse.

A consultant psychiatrist will meet and examine you. They will discuss your care and treatment with you. This examination must happen as soon as possible or, at the latest, within 24 hours of your arrival. The consultant psychiatrist will then decide if you have a mental disorder and whether or not you should stay in the hospital for treatment.

If the consultant psychiatrist believes you should stay in hospital, they will sign an **admission order**.

When the **admission order** is signed, you will become a patient of the hospital.

You will have a care team (see 'Words we use in this booklet', page 11) when you are in hospital. You can discuss your care and treatment with your care team.

If the consultant psychiatrist does not believe you have a mental disorder, they will not sign the admission order and you will be free to leave the hospital. You may discuss the option of staying in the hospital voluntarily with a member of your care team.

How long will I be kept in hospital?

An admission order lasts for 21 days. You will have a mental health tribunal hearing during this time. The mental health tribunal is a panel of people who will look at your admission to decide if the law was followed.

Most patients recover from a mental disorder within the first few weeks in hospital. Some may take longer.

What will happen after my admission order ends?

Your consultant psychiatrist will examine you in the seven days before the admission order ends. If they think that you have a mental disorder, they will sign a **renewal order**. This renewal order means that your consultant psychiatrist believes that it is in your best interest to stay in hospital for another period of time, which cannot be longer than three months.

Your case will be reviewed by a mental health tribunal (see page 59).

Your consultant psychiatrist will examine you again in the seven days before the renewal order ends. If you still have a mental disorder, they will sign another renewal order. This renewal order means that you must stay in hospital for another period of time, which cannot be longer than six months.

Again, your case will be reviewed by a mental health tribunal.

Your consultant psychiatrist will examine you again in the seven days before this second renewal order ends. If you still have a mental disorder, they will sign another renewal order. This renewal order means you must stay in hospital for a further period of time, which cannot be longer than 12 months.

A mental health tribunal will review your case every time a renewal order is made.

What are my rights when I am in hospital under an admission order or a renewal order?

Your consultant psychiatrist must do two things **within 24 hours** of signing an admission order or a renewal order.

1. They must give you a written statement saying:

   o that an admission order or a renewal order has been made;

- what type of treatment has been recommended for you;

- that you may stay in the hospital as a voluntary patient;

- that your stay will be reviewed by a mental health tribunal;

- that you have the right to a lawyer;

- that you may appeal the decision of the mental health tribunal to the Circuit Court; and

- that you may contact the Inspector of Mental Health Services (see page 74).

2. They must send a copy of the admission order or renewal order to the Mental Health Commission.

If you do not understand the information that your consultant psychiatrist gives you, ask them to explain it in more detail. You should always ask as many questions as you need to so you can fully understand your care and treatment.

What happens when the Mental Health Commission receives my admission order or renewal order?

The Mental Health Commission receives your admission order or renewal order. This contains some of your personal information such as your name, date of birth and home address. The Mental Health Commission will use this information to do three things.

1. We will organise a lawyer for you.

   This lawyer will be a barrister or a solicitor. They will meet you to help you prepare for your mental health tribunal hearing and discuss your case with you. We provide this lawyer free of charge but you do not have to use them. If you choose to use your own lawyer, however, you may have to pay their costs.

2. We will arrange for another consultant psychiatrist to visit and examine you and discuss your case with you. For more information on another consultant psychiatrist, please see 'Words we use in this booklet', page 10.

This consultant psychiatist will review any documents that your care team has about your case and meet with your consultant psychiatrist. The consultant psychiatrist we have arranged for you will then write a report about your case for the members of the mental health tribunal. Your lawyer will get a copy of the report.

3. We will arrange for your case to be reviewed by a **mental health tribunal**. For more information on the mental health tribunal, see page 59.

Questions and answers about my treatment

What is informed consent?

Consent means you agree to treatment. To give informed consent, you must fully understand what you are agreeing to.

Your consultant psychiatrist must give you information about your treatment plan. You must be able to understand that information and make a decision about it. You must also be able to tell that decision to your consultant psychiatrist. They should discuss it with you and explain why they think it will benefit you.

Your consultant psychiatrist should make sure that you understand what effects the treatment will have on you. You should also be told what might happen if you do not agree to the treatment. Your consultant psychiatrist should tell you about other methods of treatment that may be available. This information should be clear and given to you in a way that you can understand. You should have time to think about the treatment before you agree to it.

If at any stage you feel you do not fully understand why you need the treatment, or the effects of the treatment, you should ask your care team to explain it to you. It is your decision and you should only agree to treatment if you fully understand why you need it and how it may benefit you.

Can I be given treatment without my consent?

As a general rule, your consent is needed for treatment. If you are in hospital against your will, there are some circumstances under the law when you may be given certain treatment even though you have not given your consent.

Below, we outline the special rules for three forms of treatment.

Medication

As an involuntary patient, you will only be given medication without your consent if your consultant psychiatrist believes that you are unable or unwilling to give consent. Your consultant psychiatrist must also believe the medication will help you to get better.

If you have been on medication for a mental disorder for three months and your consultant psychiatrist feels that you should continue on the same type of medication, they will ask for your consent to continue the medication.

If you do not consent, they must ask a second consultant psychiatrist to authorise the medication. If the second consultant psychiatrist agrees that you should continue on the same type of medication, then you must do so for up to three months. Every three months, your medication will be reviewed in the same way, if you remain an involuntary patient.

Electro-convulsive therapy (ECT)

Electro-convulsive therapy is generally known as 'ECT'.

If you are an involuntary patient and your consultant psychiatrist thinks you need ECT, they will discuss the procedure in detail with you. You should be fully informed of what ECT is, its risks and effects. The consultant psychiatrist will then ask you to agree to it. You can ask your consultant psychiatrist any questions about ECT and its effects.

Insane →

If you do not consent to ECT, your consultant psychiatrist must ask a second consultant psychiatrist to authorise the treatment. If the second consultant psychiatrist assesses your case and agrees that ECT will help you to get better, then you will be given the treatment without your consent.

Both consultant psychiatrists must believe that the treatment is in your best interests and that it will help you to get better.

Strict rules must be followed for this treatment.

Psychosurgery

Psychosurgery is a surgical treatment that is very rarely used. It used to be known as 'lobotomy'. If your consultant psychiatrist believes it is necessary to help you get better, they will discuss the procedure with you in detail. They will also discuss the effects of the surgery.

If you consent to psychosurgery, your consultant psychiatrist will inform the Mental Health Commission of your decision. We will then ask a mental health tribunal to review your case for psychosurgery. The mental health tribunal will consider whether or not it is in your best interests. **It can only be done if you consent *and* if a mental health tribunal decides that you need it.**

Questions and answers about my stay in hospital

Can I be moved to another hospital?

Yes, you can.

The person who asked your doctor to recommend that you be admitted may also ask for you to be moved to another hospital.

Sometimes another hospital may have other treatments available that your care team thinks could improve your condition. You may be transferred to that hospital for treatment.

Here is what **must** happen before you can be moved to another hospital.

1. The clinical director of the hospital where you are staying must believe that it is in your best interests to be moved to the other hospital.

2. The clinical director of the hospital where you might be moved must agree with the move.

Can I be moved to a general hospital to receive medical treatment?

If you need general medical treatment during your stay, you may be moved to a general hospital. The clinical director of the hospital you are staying in will decide if you need to do this. You will come back to the hospital for mental health treatment when your medical treatment is finished.

Can I be moved to the Central Mental Hospital?

You can only be moved to the Central Mental Hospital if a mental health tribunal approves it.

Can I leave the hospital while I am an involuntary patient?

If you are admitted as an involuntary patient, you may want to leave the hospital from time to time. You can discuss this with any member of your care team. You should explain why you want to leave and how long you want to leave for.

Your consultant psychiatrist will consider your request to leave the hospital. They will then decide whether you can leave the hospital for the amount of time that you both agree.

If your consultant psychiatrist agrees, they will give you a note to allow you to leave the hospital. The note will let you know how long you may leave the hospital for and may also have some conditions that you must follow while you are away from the hospital. If there is anything on the note that you do not understand, you can discuss it with a member of your care team.

When you are away from the hospital, as agreed with your consultant psychiatrist, you will be **'absent with leave'**.

You must return to the hospital on or before the day and the time that the note says.

At any time during your leave, if your consultant psychiatrist thinks it is in your best interests to return, or if you break any of the conditions attached to your time away, you will be told in writing that you have to come back immediately.

If you leave without permission, or if you do not return when you are supposed to, you will be considered to be **'absent without leave'**. The staff of the hospital may bring you back to the hospital. Sometimes, they may ask the Gardaí to help them.

When can I be discharged?

You may be discharged at any time if your consultant psychiatrist believes that you no longer have a mental disorder that requires treatment in hospital. If this is the case, you will be free to leave the hospital. You can discuss this with your care team.

Your consultant psychiatrist may feel that you need to continue your treatment after you are discharged. They will discuss this with you before you leave and you should ask any questions you may have. It is very important that you understand the effects of your treatment.

If you and your consultant psychiatrist believe that you would still benefit from care and treatment in hospital, you may stay as a voluntary patient. You should discuss this with your consultant psychiatrist.

You must write to the Mental Health Commission if you are discharged before your mental health tribunal hearing but you would still like it to go ahead.

Other information

Taking part in clinical trials

The Mental Health Act 2001 does not allow any person who is admitted involuntarily with a mental disorder (see page 22 for the definition of a mental disorder) to take part in clinical trials. A clinical trial means a test of new treatments.

Bodily restraint and seclusion

There may be times when you have to be physically restrained or placed in seclusion while in a hospital. This will only happen if your care team thinks it is absolutely necessary, for example to prevent you injuring yourself or someone else. This may also apply to voluntary patients.

Strict rules must be followed by anyone who attempts to physically restrain you (to hold you down or force you to stay in one place) or put you in seclusion (make you stay on your own).

Mental health tribunals

What is a mental health tribunal?

Under the Act, everyone who is involuntarily admitted is reviewed by a mental health tribunal. This is a group of three people who will look at your admission to decide if it followed the law and will make sure that your rights are protected.

The Mental Health Commission will make sure that you are only detained and treated in a hospital under the rules set out in the Act.

If the mental health tribunal decides that you do not meet the conditions for involuntary admission, they will make sure that you are discharged. You may continue to stay in hospital as a voluntary patient.

Who sits on a mental health tribunal?

There are a number of independent people throughout the country who work on mental health tribunals.

Each mental health tribunal is made up of three people:

- a chairperson (who is a barrister or a solicitor);

- a consultant psychiatrist (who is not your consultant psychiatrist); and

- a lay person (who is not a registered medical practitioner or registered nurse or one of the above).

What do mental health tribunals review?

Mental health tribunals review:

- admission orders;

- renewal orders;

- certain transfer orders;

- proposals for psychosurgery; and

- patients who were being detained under the Mental Treatment Act 1945 when the Mental Health Act 2001 took effect.

How do I bring my case before a mental health tribunal if I am admitted involuntarily?

If you are admitted involuntarily, your case is automatically referred to a mental health tribunal. The consultant psychiatrist who signed your admission order will inform the Mental Health Commission about your admission within 24 hours of signing the admission form.

The Mental Health Commission will automatically appoint a lawyer to represent you, free of charge, at the mental health tribunal hearing. If you choose your own lawyer, you may have to pay their fees.

We will automatically arrange for another consultant psychiatrist (see 'Words we use in this booklet', page 10) to examine you.

How do I bring my case to a mental health tribunal if I am detained under a renewal order?

If your stay has been extended by a renewal order, your consultant psychiatrist will inform us. They will do this within 24 hours of signing the renewal form. We will then automatically arrange a mental health tribunal hearing to review the renewal order in the same way that your admission order was reviewed. You are entitled to a review every time a renewal order is made.

How will I know when the mental health tribunal is ready to hear my case?

The Mental Health Commission will contact you and your lawyer to let you know where and when the review will take place.

If you have just been admitted, the review must take place within 21 days of your admission. If you are in hospital under a renewal order, the review must take place within 21 days of the renewal order of the order being made.

The review will usually be held in a private area of the hospital you are staying in.

The mental health tribunal will contact your consultant psychiatrist. The mental health tribunal will also look at all the records of your stay in the hospital. This will include the independent report of the consultant psychiatrist who was sent by the Mental Health Commission to examine you. You or your lawyer will be given copies of all documents and reports. You can discuss these with your lawyer or your care team. This may help you to prepare for your hearing.

If I am discharged or become a voluntary patient before my mental health tribunal hearing, can I still have a hearing?

You can have a mental health tribunal hearing if you are discharged or if you become a voluntary patient. You **must** inform us in writing, **within 14 days** of your discharge or your decision to become a voluntary patient, if you would like your mental health tribunal hearing to go ahead.

What actually happens at the mental health tribunal hearing?

The hearing is held in private. The members of the mental health tribunal will have read the reports about your case. You and your lawyer will also have copies of those reports.

The mental health tribunal *must* see:

○ your admission or renewal forms; and

○ the medical report from the consultant psychiatrist who carried out an independent medical examination.

At the hearing, you will be able to speak to the members of the mental health tribunal. You can discuss any aspect of your admission to hospital with them. Your lawyer may stay with you while you discuss these issues. If you prefer, your lawyer may discuss your case with the mental health tribunal for you.

The mental health tribunal members may ask to speak to people who are involved in your care in hospital or to anyone involved in your admission process. These people are called witnesses. Any witness who speaks at the mental health tribunal can be questioned by you or your lawyer.

You have the right to be at the hearing, but you do not have to attend if you don't want to. You can discuss this with your lawyer and your care team. Your lawyer can present your case for you.

If you do not attend the hearing, your lawyer will still be there to present your case, look after your interests and protect your rights.

How does the mental health tribunal make a decision?

The three members of the mental health tribunal will carefully consider everything they have heard and the reports they have read.

The mental health tribunal reviews:

○ all the information about your admission and stay in hospital;

○ the views that you and your lawyer have presented; and

○ the views of any witnesses at the hearing.

If two or three members of the mental health tribunal believe that the procedures for involuntary admission followed the law and that you need to stay in the hospital, their decision will be to **affirm the admission** or **renewal order**.

If two or three members of the mental health tribunal believe that the procedures for involuntary admission did not follow the law and that you do not need to stay in the hospital, their decision will be to **revoke the admission** or **renewal order**.

You will be told the decision of the mental health tribunal as soon as possible. The tribunal will also tell their decision to your consultant psychiatrist and your lawyer. They may write to anyone else they think should know the outcome of the hearing, for example your GP or carer.

1

What if the mental health tribunal decides that I should not be detained?

If the mental health tribunal decides that you should no longer be involuntarily admitted, you will be free to leave the hospital. You can discuss this with your care team. It may be possible for you to stay in the hospital as a voluntary patient.

What can I do if I disagree with the mental health tribunal's decision?

You may be able to appeal the decision to the Circuit Court on the grounds that you are not suffering from a mental disorder. You must make the appeal within 14 days of the mental health tribunal's decision. If you are not happy with the decision of the Circuit Court, you should discuss this with your lawyer.

Mental Health Commission
and the
Inspector of
Mental Health Services

Mental Health Commission

What is the Mental Health Commission?

We are an independent statutory organisation. That means that we are established by law, in this case the Mental Health Act 2001. We receive funding from the Government but do not take direction from any outside organisation.

We have two important jobs:

- to make sure that mental health services maintain the high standards and good practices set out in the law; and

- to protect the interests of people using mental health services.

71

The Commission is a group of 13 people appointed by the Minister for Health and Children. We are made up of people with a wide range of experience and expertise in mental health issues from:

- medicine;

- law;

- nursing;

- social work;

- clinical psychology;

- voluntary bodies that promote mental health issues (including mental health service users); and

- the general public.

What do we do?

The day-to-day running of the organisation is carried out by an executive team. The executive team cannot include Commission members. There are six members on the executive team and a number of support staff to help them with their work.

To promote high standards and good practices in the mental health services, we carry out checks to make sure that:

- hospitals are properly managed and run in line with the law and provide a high standard of mental health care (they can only be on our list of approved centres if they meet these standards);

- the Mental Health Act 2001 is working properly to protect your rights; and

- mental health services in the community provide the highest standard of care.

Inspector of Mental Health Services

The Mental Health Commission appoints the Inspector of Mental Health Services. The inspector must be a consultant psychiatrist. The inspector works with a number of assistant inspectors. The assistant inspectors come from various backgrounds, including nursing, social work, occupational therapy, psychiatry and clinical psychology.

What does the Inspector of Mental Health Services do?

The inspector and assistant inspectors:

- visit approved centres where people are detained and treated;

- make sure that mental health services are providing quality mental health care in line with the law; and

○ carry out a review of the quality of mental health services and prepare a written report. This is called the report of the Inspector of Mental Health Services, and is included in the annual report of the Mental Health Commission.

If you would like to meet the inspector during their visit, you should ask a member of your care team to set up a meeting.

Support organisations

Alzheimer Society of Ireland

The Alzheimer Society of Ireland was established by a group of carers to provide support and services to people with dementia and their carers.

Temple Road, Blackrock, Co. Dublin

Information Line: 1800 341 341

Telephone: (01) 207 3800 **Fax:** (01) 210 3772

Web: www.alzheimer.ie

Email: info@alzheimer.ie

Aware

Aware is a voluntary organisation of patients, relatives and mental health professionals whose aim is to help people affected by depression.

72 Lower Leeson Street, Dublin 2

Information Line: 1890 303 302

Telephone: (01) 661 7211 **Fax:** (01) 661 7217

Web: www.aware.ie

Email: info@aware.ie

GROW

GROW is a mental health organisation that helps people who have suffered, or are suffering, from mental health problems. Members are helped to both prevent and recover from mental breakdown. GROW's principal strength is the support members give each other.

Grow Office, Barrack Street, Co. Kilkenny

Information Line: 1890 474 474

Telephone: (056) 776 1624

Fax: (056) 775 1615

Web: www.grow.ie

Email: info@grow.ie

Irish Advocacy Network

The Irish Advocacy Network exists to promote and facilitate peer advocacy on an island wide basis. This is achieved through the provision of information and support for mental health service users and or survivors. The network aims to support people in speaking up for themselves and in achieving empowerment by taking control of their own lives.

Health Care Unit, Rooskey, Monaghan, Co. Monaghan

Telephone: (047) 38918 **Fax:** (047) 38682

Web: www.irishadvocacynetwork.com

Email: admin@irishadvocacynetwork.com

Mental Health Ireland

Mental Health Ireland promotes positive mental health and supports people with a mental illness, their families and carers, by identifying their needs and advocating for their rights.

Mensana House, 6 Adelaide Street, Dun Laoghaire, Co. Dublin

Telephone: (01) 284 1166 **Fax:** (01) 284 1736

Web: www.mentalhealthireland.ie

Email: information@mentalhealthireland.ie

H.S.E. Information Line

1800 111 888.

Rights

01 636 2400,

Shine – Supporting People Affected by Mental Ill Health

Shine supports people with mental ill health and their families and friends. Shine does this by promoting and providing high quality services and by working to improve the quality of life of the people it serves.

38 Blessington Street, Dublin 7

Helpline: 1890 621 631

Telephone: (01) 860 1620 **Fax:** (01) 860 1602

Web: www.shineonline.ie *and* www.recover.ie

Email: info@shineonline.ie

1800 111 888.

086 01 44 212
086 852